Book 1
Malware
By Solis Tech

&

Book 2
CompTIA A+
By Solis Tech

Book 1
Malware
By Solis Tech

Malware Detection & Threats Made Easy!

Malware: Malware Detection & Threats Made Easy!

Table of Contents

Introduction

I want to thank you and congratulate you for purchasing the book, *"Malware: Malware Detection & Threats Made Easy!"*.

This book contains proven steps and strategies on how to avoid, detect and remove malware.

Malware creators are very creative, employing both technical and social means to spread malware. Simply installing antivirus software is no longer enough. This book explains how malware spreads in order to arm the reader with information on how to manage its threat.

Thanks again for purchasing this book, I hope you enjoy it!

Chapter 1 – Malware

Computers are inherently dumb. They can accept and input data, can process it at high-speed, and can return the results almost instantly. However, users need to tell the computer what to do in the form of codes. We call these codes programs, applications, scripts or software, but they are essentially the same. They give instructions to the computer. What the computer does will depend on the instructions given to it. Tell it to do something useful and it will. Give it instructions to perform a malicious task and it will do it without question. Even computers with artificial intelligence are simply following instructions that simulate human's way of thinking.

Computers do not care who gives the instructions. As long as the instructions are loaded into memory, the computer will process it accordingly. Upon startup, a short set of instructions will tell the computer to load and launch the operating system or OS. The OS in turn executes startup instructions that it finds. These include preparing the input and output drivers, as well as launching other background tasks. Having done that, the OS awaits command from its user to execute other applications.

Malware developers take advantage of these key concepts. They find vulnerabilities in the operating and network system that will allow them to install malware and have it running in the background. Vulnerabilities are bugs in the program that can let malware writers load additional code and execute it. These bugs or programming errors do not always appear during the testing stage.

Some malware writers use social engineering to trick victims into installing malware into their computers. They use the computer's connection to internal and external networks to propagate the malware. They infect shared storage to spread malware among colleagues. They hack into servers to install malicious code that will infect site visitors. They can do this because computers will run any executable code that is loaded into its memory.

What is Malware?

Malware is short for malicious software. It is a general term for a code that compromises a computer and instructs it to do malicious tasks, often without the knowledge or permission from the computer's owner. Early malware refers to programming challenges and pranks like programs that delete user files, but recent malware refers to targeting servers to make them inaccessible or for financial gains.

Home computers are not safe, either. Cybercriminals are using home computers to launch attacks on servers in addition to stealing personal information to access online bank accounts. Some advertisers adopt malware, too. They no longer wait for users to visit their sites, but install malware into a victim's computer so they can modify browser settings and change the default home page, eventually advertising their products every time a user opens the browser. They sometimes change the default search engine, replacing it with engines that track user habits to benefit advertisers.

Mobile devices are not safe, either. Today's mobile devices are computers with features and capabilities that are comparable to older computers. Mobile devices, like smartphones and tablets, are vulnerable because they require applications to work. If users inadvertently download a compromised application, then there is a possibility that malware can compromise their mobile devices, too.

A future malware playground is Internet of Things. It is a term for consumer devices like smart home appliances and vehicles loaded with small computers to provide intelligent functionality. These intelligent appliances connect to the Internet for remote control and administration. Having computers on these things, it may not be long until we can see malware on these devices too.

Remember that appliance manufacturers are not IT companies; hence, they may not have the capability to implement data security in their products. A hacker compromising a manufacturer's server could trigger a firmware update on connected appliances and make it perform additional functions, including attacking other servers on the Internet. It may sound like an event from a science-fiction movie, but this reality is possible.

What is the Difference Between a Malware and a Virus?

Many people confuse malware with viruses. A virus is a type of malware, while malware include viruses and other malicious software.

The first malware were viruses, and developers wrote antivirus software to eliminate these malicious programs. Even when viruses evolved to other forms, people still call them viruses and antivirus companies are using the same term even if they are targeting other malware variants.

Viruses are no longer common on their original form. With antivirus vendors constantly updating their algorithms, malware developers have to come up with new variants to avoid detection, often employing social engineering to propagate malware faster by tricking victims to install it along with legitimate software.

If we look at how malware developers remain active over the years, we can surmise that it is a financially rewarding business; therefore, we can expect cybercriminals to continue developing better malware while antivirus companies play catch-up. The only way to combat malware is to understand the threat it presents, how it spreads and propagates, how to detect it, and how to remove.

What are Potentially Unwanted Programs (PUPs)?

People love free software; however, developers need to earn money too. Malware developers see this as an opportunity to spread malware while providing revenue to free-software developers. What they come up with are installers for legitimate software that also install malware during installation. Antivirus companies call these Potentially Unwanted Programs instead of malware since victims give explicit permission to install them. They have no way of knowing if users allow the installation on purpose or unknowingly installs them.

Why would Users Give Permission to Install PUPs?

Most users do not bother reading user agreements that installers display during installation. Instead, they simply click on the default buttons or press enter. Even if users will read the agreements and prompts, some may not understand the message and assume that they are installing software that is necessary for the main program to work. Unfortunately, PUPs are easy to install, but are often frustrating to remove from the system. Most have more than one instance running such that removing a copy will trigger the second copy to re-install it. Many recent PUPs affect users' browsers, which can be very annoying.

How to Detect the Presence of Malware?

Users familiar with their computer will sometimes notice unusual behavior. Some are obvious, like the browser's looks suddenly changing. Other users may lose their files or the file types are changed. Users may even see system errors that were not present before.

Some changes are not visual, like a program accessing the hard disk and making noise even when the computer is idle. Malware accessing an external server can slow down Internet connection. Infected computers can also be unresponsive when hidden processes are running and using up the computer's memory.

Before assuming that malware may be causing the problem, try restarting the computer and leave it for a few minutes without running any program. If the computer is still slow, then there may be an unwanted background program running, but it still needs confirmation.

On Windows, check the hard disk space by opening any folder and clicking Computer on the left. A hard disk with very little space can slow down the computer and malware may not be the cause.

If there is plenty of hard disk space available, run the Task Manager by holding Ctrl+Alt+Del and selecting it from the menu. Click on the Performance tab and observe the real-time graph. Both the CPU and memory usage should be relatively flat if the computer is idle. An active graph could mean that a hidden program is busy. Click the Applications tab to confirm. There should be no application listed if the user did not execute a program. If there is no program listed and the CPU or memory graph is active then there could be a malware running in the background.

To see the process that is using up the memory, click on the Process tab, then click Memory to display the list in descending order. Check its Image name and description. Right-click on a name, then select Properties to get more details. Use a search engine to validate suspicious names.

The Networking tab can also give clues on the presence of malware. There should be no network activity if the computer is idle. If the network is slow and this graph is active, then a hidden program is accessing an external server or computer.

These are just some ways of detecting the possible presence of malware. Without knowing what the malware exactly is; however, it could be difficult to remove it manually.

Most leading antivirus software can detect and remove malware. For home users, there are free versions available that offer basic protection with the option to purchase upgrades for additional features.

A Note on USB flash drives

With the popularity of USB flash drives, spreading malware via USB is easier. Malware can automatically execute when the user opens a USB flash drive. Once in computer memory, inserting another USB drive will infect it. To prevent this, do not view the contents of a USB flash drive after it mounts. Instead, right-click on the drive's name or icon, then select the scan option from the antivirus. This will remove malware in the flash drive before using it.

If there are signs that a USB drive is infected, but the antivirus does not detect it, install another antivirus program. Some antivirus solutions are not good at detecting USB-based malware.

Antivirus solutions can prevent the installation of malware to some extent. However, there are malware that can still get through if the user is not aware of how they propagate. The best way to prevent malware from infecting computers is to understand how each type works.

The succeeding chapters give an insight into the various forms of malware. It also provides information on how they spread so that users can avoid infecting their computers. Prevention is still the best cure against malware. However, avoiding malware is not easy.

Chapter 2 – Virus

Viruses are the earliest forms of malware and they date back to the time before personal computers became popular. A virus is simply a program that can replicate itself on the same computer. Even without malicious intent, creating many copies of a virus code can quickly fill up the memory and slow the computer down. However, an unmodified virus cannot spread to other computers by itself even if the computers are on a network. Getting the virus inside a computer is the challenge for virus creators.

To avoid detection, virus creators modify legitimate programs by inserting malicious codes. When these programs launch, the virus loads into memory and scans the computer for other executable codes to infect. The virus code stays active in memory until the computer shuts down and the cycle starts again if the user runs the infected program.

Boot Sector Virus

Some viruses attack the boot sector of the computer's bootable disks. The boot sector is an area of a disk that a disk drive initially reads and loads into memory. It contains the startup code that will load other components of the operating system. When the boot sector is infected, the virus loads into memory every time the computer starts, ensuring that it is active without waiting for the user to run an infected program. Since the disk operating system can fit in diskettes in the early days of personal computers, starting a clean computer with an infected bootable diskette can also spread the virus to that computer.

Be Careful when Using Shared Resources

Viruses can spread through sharing. When a user mounts a removable storage media on an infected computer while a virus is active, the virus attempts to infect programs that it finds on the mounted media as well. In the early days, this applies to floppy diskettes and external hard drives, but infections are more common today on flash USB drives.

Once the user connects an infected storage to another computer and runs an infected program, the virus activates and infects the other programs in the new computer as well. This makes users who mount USB drives on shared computers at risk if the computer has no sufficient antivirus protection installed. For this reason, avoid connecting USB drives at Internet cafes and on other public computers.

Even shared documents can carry viruses. Some productivity software allows scripts or macros to automate common tasks. Scripts and macros are small, but powerful programs; hence, they can spread viruses, too. Executing an infected macro will also compromise other documents on the same computer. Worse, sending a copy of an infected document can also infect the receiver's computer.

Are Early Viruses Malicious?

Some early viruses started as programming challenges. There was a game that was named Core Wars where the objective is to create a program that loads in memory, then replicate and terminate other programs running on the same memory space. The competing programs create copies of the code while overwriting enemy codes to terminate them. The program that remains in control is the winner.

Other early versions are simply annoying. Two programmers wrote the Brain virus because users were illegally copying their diskettes. The Brain virus simply displays information about the programmers. The Brain virus spread to computers in other countries.

Computers were not widely connected before and the worst thing that a virus can do is to delete files or make them inaccessible. This is exactly what early destructive viruses did. Some programmers wrote viruses that display something interesting while deleting computer files.

Birth of Antivirus Companies

It was not long before other programmers started writing codes to remove viruses, turning the process into a never-ending game of cat and mouse. Virus creators are continually discovering new computer vulnerabilities that they can take advantage of, while antivirus developers update their codes to combat new virus strains. It has become a never ending battle between malware developers and antivirus companies.

Antivirus programs initially identify specific viruses using their signatures. Signatures are like patterns or fingerprints that identify specific viruses. Virus creators responded by continually creating virus variants that require new methods of detection to keep up. This is why antivirus programs update their databases almost daily.

Antivirus can only play catch up if they rely solely on signatures. Modern antivirus programs detect possible viruses by their behavior in addition to signatures.

Most free antivirus software in the market can eliminate common virus threats so not having one installed is not an excuse. While they retain the name, current antivirus software can detect and remove other forms of malware. To enable additional protection, users can purchase additional features.

However, those who do not have a budget for paid features can still protect themselves from malware. The key is to understand how other forms of malware spread. The next chapters will explain these.

Chapter 3 - Worms

While viruses were a threat due to their ability to replicate, it is not a tool for mass infection because it cannot spread to other computers. The capability to spread over the network by itself is a feature of worms. Networks include local area networks (LAN) that are commonly found in offices, Wide Area Network (WAN) for remote offices, as well as worldwide networks like the Internet.

Early worm research had good intentions and started as helpful ideas. One worm crawls networked computers at night to run processor-intensive tasks, but saves the work and stays idle during the day so people can use the computers normally. It is a good idea that maximizes computer resources, similar to how modern cloud computing works. However, a programming error caused the computers to crash and they had to write another program to remove it.

Another programmer wrote a seemingly harmless worm to check the size of the Internet. The worm creates copies on target computers as it moved from one computer to the next. Due to a programming decision, it can install a copy even if it already exists on the same computer. Multiple running copies of the same worm can slow down the computer until it eventually crashes. A single worm was able to crash a big part the Internet.

Worms spread across the network by exploiting operating system and application vulnerabilities and taking advantage of insufficient data security practices. Nowadays, worms can also spread through social engineering. Social engineering is a technique used by hackers to trick users into unknowingly breaking standard data security precautions. Hackers can bypass a highly secure environment using social engineering.

Operating systems, or OS, are programs that manage computers and network equipment. Just like any program, it can have unintentional bugs and updating usually fixes the problem. Worms take advantage of these vulnerabilities to compromise the system.

If the OS or application developer releases an update before someone announces the vulnerability, then users have time to update the operating system before a malware exploits the vulnerability. This is why users should install updates especially if the patch is to address data security issues. Allowing automatic updates usually takes care of this, although there is a risk of automatically installing buggy updates.

On the other hand, if a malware creator releases a worm before the developer discovers the bug and releases an update, what we have is zero-day vulnerability. Modern antivirus companies address this by developing algorithms that detect malicious behavior. However, very aggressive antivirus solutions may lead to false positives.

False positives result when a scan reports the presence of malicious code when there is none. A good antivirus has few false positives. Third party evaluations can determine effective antivirus solutions with fewer false positives.

Mass-mailer worms

Worms can access email clients on user computers and use it to email copies of the worm to contacts in the address book. Some of these emails can trick recipients into downloading and installing the attachment, compromising the receiver's computer in the process. When this happens, that computer also becomes a mass-mailing tool. Unfortunately, these worms can also get a name from the address book and change the From field with this name. This means that the sender in the email may not be the email source, making the source difficult to track.

Aside from possibly compromising recipients' computers, mass mailers can also slow down network performance. If a worm infects several computers on the same network, then it could eat up all the allocated bandwidth. Worse, data security companies may include the computer's IP address in the blacklist for spamming. This can affect all computers in the network that shares the same public IP.

This is because most offices and home networks use a single public IP address for their router while individual computers get private IP addresses. Worse, some DSL subscribers may get a banned public IP address when their router restarts.

Always be wary of unsolicited emails with attachment even if it comes from a trusted source. A possible indicator of spam mail is when the receiver's name is not mentioned in the salutation. Bad grammar is also a sign of possible spam email.

Do not assume that the antivirus can catch all worm variants. Some worms change the file extension of the attached file. Users may think that they are opening an image file when in reality they are executing a worm. Worms do this by adding a .jpg to the filename, like picture.jpg.exe. Since many users configure their computers to hide the file extension, they do not see that the real extension is .exe because the filename they see is picture.jpg.

Some mass-mailer worms simply send spam advertisements. While they may not do damage to a user's computer, they can still trick victims into purchasing illegitimate products. These emails often have a web beacon, a small image that is loaded from an external server. Displaying this image will send the user's email address to the server, thereby validating that it is an active email account. It will then be a target for future spam emails.

Note that spammers do not use their own computers to send mass emails. They use email worms to prevent authorities from easily tracking them.

Worms for Phishing

Mass-mailer worms provide a great platform for quickly distributing malware. Malware creators use these worms to transport different payloads depending on their intention. One application of mass-mailers is for phishing.

Phishing is a form of identity fraud and is usually for stealing personal information for financial gains. It works this way.

Malware creators will copy a legitimate website's looks, specifically the login and profile pages. Websites of financial institutions like banks and payment platforms are examples of these. Next, they will create an email that looks like an official document coming from the target institutions. These emails often have a sense of urgency, requiring the user to log in to the website immediately to validate or change the password for security purposes. It will also include a link to the appropriate page for the user's convenience.

There lies the trick. Instead of linking to the legitimate page, it will redirect the user to the fake login page after clicking the email link. The URL will have the legitimate website's domain name, but with added characters. Some users may mistakenly believe that they are in the genuine site and proceed to log in. After entering the login detail, the next page may even require them to enter their credit card details for validation.

In reality, users can enter anything in the login page and it will be successful. The login page will simply save the credentials entered by the user, then display a page to get other credentials. When in doubt, users can initially enter incorrect login credentials to check if the site can really validate their account. If it accepts a wrong username or password, then there is no validation and the site is a fake.

Another way to verify if a website is a fake is through browsing all the menus and internal links before entering the login details. Malware creators may not go through the trouble of recreating an entire website's content.

To guard against phishing, never click on an email link to log in or change account details. Always type the known URL on the browser address bar. If clicking an email link asks the user to log in, then do not continue. Instead, type the correct URL in the browser's address bar before logging in.

The next chapter discusses other payloads that worms usually bring.

Chapter 4 - Trojan Horse

Trojans are malware that disguise as useful programs or install together with a legitimate application. Its name comes from the Trojan War, a part of Greek mythology where a wooden gift horse had soldiers inside that attacked the enemies while they were asleep to win the war. Similarly, a Trojan pretends to be a useful application, waiting for the user to launch it to execute the malicious code. Once activated, trojans will run in the background to do their designated task.

Trojans do not replicate and spread by themselves. They often combine with worms to infect other computers. Trojans are also common on unsolicited email attachments, while some users download them along with valid applications.

There are several types of trojans according to function.

Root kits

Root kit is not inherently bad. It is originally a tool for system administrators. It becomes bad if the creator installs it on a computer without permission from the owner, especially if the purpose is to do malicious tasks.

Some trojans will modify the computer's system for hackers to gain access. Root kits are tools for administrators that hide in the operating system while providing a back door for their creator. With privileged access, a root kit's owner can do almost anything to the infected computer remotely. Root kits are good at hiding their existence, making them difficult to detect. They can also delete any traces of malware installation. Root kits usually remain hidden until activated.

Bots

Bots are programs that perform automated tasks. Some bots, called spambots, flood websites with spam advertisements to generate traffic for another website. This is common in online forums and is the main reason why websites validate users before accepting their registration details. Some registration forms require the user to type the characters shown on an image to validate that the applicant is human. However, some spammers go around this by hiring humans to solve the test, although it comes at a cost.

A more malicious bot is one that employs brute-force attack on target websites. Most website owners do not build websites from scratch, but simply use an open source Content Management System (CMS) as a starting point. A CMS is a fully functioning website that allows the user to update content without writing a single line of HTML code. There are many templates to choose from, and websites owners can customize further by using their own graphic images. Using CMS, owners can update website content in a few clicks.

Many CMS software have the default username "admin" and some website owners do not bother changing it. Given the default administrator name, hackers only need to guess the password to take over the website and install malicious software. If it is a popular forum, then there is a risk that hackers can steal the member database.

To attack a website, hackers write bots that log into the target website and try to log in with passwords taken from a table of common passwords as well as words from the dictionary. A website that does not limit failed logins in a given period is a good target. Using a network of zombie computers, hackers are able to brute-force attack a website using bots with minimal risk of authorities tracking the attack's mastermind.

Stolen password databases from forums are not safe, either. Using rainbow tables, hackers can use brute-force to find the matching password for a member account. Since many users employ the same username and password on all sites they register to, this allows the hackers to hack into members' accounts on other sites as well.

Remote-controlled Bots

Malware developers can turn an infected computer into a remote-controlled bot that will perform malicious tasks, including attacking another computer. This is how they get away with Distributed Denial of Service attacks. Attackers do not use their own computers to flood a server, but instead, they use a large network of zombie computers from unsuspecting users. This also saves the attacker from bandwidth costs since the computer owner is paying for it. It also makes it difficult to track the attacker after it spreads from one computer to another.

One analysis of an affected computer shows that bots log into a chat server, waiting for commands from its master. Think of an army of sleeper bots just waiting patiently for a command to attack. Developers will typically just let an installed Trojan do nothing until they have an army of remote-controlled bots to launch a large-scale cyber-attack. The attacker then issues the command to attack from the chat server where the bots log in each time the infected computer is running.

Without good anti-malware software, the presence of a remote-controlled bot in a computer is difficult to detect since it sleeps until a command is given.

Keylogger

Some trojans can capture keystrokes as well as mouse movements in the background without the user knowing it. Called keyloggers, these programs can serve as surveillance software for a good purpose. Some parents use it to monitor children's online activity.

Trojan keyloggers can steal passwords and other personal credentials from unsuspecting users. It can wait for specific events, like users opening a login page, before starting to record user actions and keystrokes. It then sends the log to a remote server for its master.

Spyware

Spyware is another Trojan that collects sensitive information similar to a keylogger. However, it is not limited to monitoring key strokes to steal user credentials, but can also gather information about the user's online activity as well.

Adware

Adware is similar to spyware, but simply records and sends users' online activity and behavior as marketing data to marketers so they can display an appropriate advertisement. Some versions will redirect browser searches to advertisements while others will replace the default search engine with an advertiser's search engine.

Adware creators write these malware for revenue generation. Adware that alters browser settings is very difficult to remove. Antivirus software can remove adware from the computer, but usually leaves the modified browser settings. Saving browser bookmarks and restoring to factory settings can sometimes fix the problem.

Ransomware

Ransomware does what its name suggests. After installing the malicious code, it will either prevent access to the infected computer or encrypt the contents of its hard disk. Users will see a message demanding payment to disable the malware. The criminals behind typically employ money transfer services that are difficult to track. Add this to the fact that these cybercriminals usually live in other countries, making it difficult to run after them.

To spread ransomware, cybercriminals typically take over a legitimate website, usually without the owner's knowledge, to install the malware. They can also spread ransomware using drive-by downloads on the compromised website.

Drive-by Download

A drive-by download will allow the installation of malware by simply browsing an infected website. The user does not even have to click a download link. The affected website contains codes that check for browser or operating system vulnerabilities that allow for automatic download. The malware will install a program with a task to connect to another server to download the rest of the malware. The victim may not notice the download due to the initial programs' small size.

Some anti-malware software can warn if a website has malware when a user tries to access it.

Suspicious Packers

In order to avoid detection, suspicious packers compress and encrypt malware code. Good anti-malware utilities are aware of this and are able to detect the behavior of suspicious packers and prevent them from executing.

Removing Trojans

Most antivirus companies have software that can automatically remove trojans. While it is possible to remove Trojans manually, this may be a challenge since many have multiple copies running that can reinstall copies if the user deletes one.

When looking for good antivirus software, try the demo versions first. If satisfied, users can pay for other features that provide complete protection to the computer. Some of these protections include email and web surfing security.

In some cases, antivirus software can remove malware from the system, but not from the browser. If removing browser add-ons and restoring to factory setting does not work, uninstall the browser and download again.

Avoiding Installer Trojans

Among the popular sources of Trojans are free software installers. Software development costs money, and offering it free is not good for business. However, many people would prefer free over paid versions, especially when performing simple or one-time tasks. To address this, developers break down their programs by specific features, then allow third party marketers to offer them as free downloads in return for revenue to the developer. For example, one utility can convert AVI formats to MP4, while another can convert MP4 to MPG.

How can marketers earn money from offering free downloads? They get revenue by offering their services to advertisers. These marketers create installers for legitimate software, then include the option to install software from other companies. There is nothing wrong with that right, except that many users do not bother reading what they are installing. Unfortunately, many of these optional programs are adware that antivirus software tag as Potential Unwanted Programs (PUP).

An installer for free software will first confirm that users want to install the desired legitimate program. After the user clicks on the Continue or Next button, the installer will get the user's consent to install additional software along with a few descriptions of its benefits. Sometimes, the installer will display an End User License Agreement (EULA), something that no one ever reads, but simply agrees to. It is common to see more than one program added in the installation. The problem, however, is that the default buttons will install these extra programs if the user is not careful.

How can users avoid these additional installations, especially if the user is unsure if the other software is required? Most installers have a Decline button for optional installations. When an installer shows the Decline button, then that additional software is probably a PUP. Pay attention to the presence of Decline buttons.

Some installers have no separate dialog boxes for additional software installation. Instead, easy and custom install options are available, with the easy install as the default. What the user may not see is that the easy install option will sometimes install additional software. Click the custom install option when it is available and deselect unfamiliar applications.

Some antivirus may give an alert that the installer has a Trojan. Always scan the installer after downloading. Users can do this by selecting the installer, right clicking then selecting the Scan option to run the antivirus. This is also a good practice after inserting USB devices.

Users can perform additional verification after each installation. In Windows, simply select Programs and Features from the control panel, then click the Installed On tab. Sort the list in descending order. The programs with the current date are the ones included in the installation. Select suspicious programs and click uninstall. To verify applications, enter the program name in a search engine to see what it does.

Chapter 5 – Threats on Mobile Devices

Mobile technology is now a part of people's everyday lives. Smartphones today are very powerful. They are no longer just for voice and text, but for accessing the Internet and playing games as well. Though not as efficient as personal computers, users can perform most tasks on their smartphones.

For those who require laptop capability at more portable form factor, tablets are a blessing. Those who want the small size of a phone, but with a bigger screen like a tablet, can choose a phablet. Mobile computing is now a reality.

As computers, these mobile devices can be targets of malware. To minimize these, Android and IOS, the leading mobile platforms, have screening policies in place to reduce the chances of malware getting into the official stores. Additionally, updates to the operating system often include security fixes for known vulnerabilities to strengthen the security of devices. Installing the latest updates, when available to the user's mobile device, addresses possible malware problems.

By default, users can only download apps from the official stores. This is Google Play for Android and App Store for IOS. However, a checkbox on Android's setting will allow the user to download from any external server. There lies the problem.

The price for mobile apps is quite low compared to their PC counterparts. However, many users still do not wish to pay for the apps they download, despite their low prices. Malware creators take advantage of this by making commercial apps available for free download on third party servers. By simply deselecting a default Android setting, users can now download a paid app for free.

Unfortunately, for them, these modified apps may contain malware written for mobile devices. Once installed on a mobile device and executed, these malware take over the device and do what PC malware often do. Some malware may steal user credentials while others may display unwanted advertisements. These malware can make the devices very slow, rendering them unusable. Restoring to factory settings may be the only option for some.

IOS has no checkbox to allow downloading of apps from unofficial sites, but bugs in the operating systems can allow jailbreaks. Jailbreaks are IOS hacks that allow users to customize their devices. It also allows users to install unofficial apps. Some of these apps may have malware and can compromise the device.

Malware creators are smart and can always find ways around a secure system. One company created a Windows application that allows users to download apps for free then transfer them to their IOS device. This comes with a risk, however, since some of these apps may also have malware.

Malware creators started targeting IOS developers in China. They did this by making local copies of Apple's development platform since downloading from Apple's official servers is quite slow for developers located in China. Unfortunately, the unofficial installer has malware that infects the apps they are developing. Some of these apps made their way into the App Store before they were discovered and removed.

Another malware creator took advantage of enterprise certificates. These certificates are used by companies to install their own apps on IOS devices without approval from Apple. Malware creators are tricking users to install an enterprise certificate so they can install apps with malware on victims' devices. Many users who do not understand the implications are at risk.

Apple quickly released an update to IOS that prevents this malware from installing. Those who are still using an older version of IOS can also avoid this malware by not allowing the installation of certificates unless it is from their company's IT department.

For IOS users, downloading apps only from the App Store can minimize the risk of malware. It does not mean that Android users are safer, though. Malware writers are invading Google Play by creating fake apps that mimic original apps, but with additional malware. Google has to monitor millions of apps and ensuring that apps do not have malware is not easy. There is a way to avoid potential malware, though. If an Android app asks for unnecessary permissions during installation, do not install it.

Fortunately, antivirus companies now have versions for both the IOS and Android platforms. Installing these apps will help users screen potential malware during installation, as well as remove malware that were accidentally installed.

Conclusion

Thank you again for purchasing this book!

I hope this book was able to help you understand malware threats to prevent them from spreading.

The next step is to check your computers for signs of malware and apply the lessons in this book to avoid infections in the future.

Finally, if you enjoyed this book, please take the time to share your thoughts and post a review on Amazon. It'd be greatly appreciated!

Thank you and good luck!

Book 2
CompTIA A+

By Solis Tech

All-in-One Certification Exam Guide for Beginners!

Table Of Contents

Introduction

I want to thank you and congratulate you for purchasing the book, *"CompTIA A+: All-in-One Certification Exam Guide for Beginners!"*

This book contains proven steps and strategies on how to prepare for the CompTIA A+ exams.

This eBook will explain the basics of the CompTIA A+ certification and tests. It will also give you some pointers regarding the topics that you need to review. By reading this book, you will gain the knowledge and skills required to pass the tests.

Thanks again for purchasing this book, I hope you enjoy it!

Chapter 1: The CompTIA A+ Examination

This eBook is written for people who are knowledgeable about computers. It assumes that you know to how to use a computer and its peripherals (e.g. printers, modems, etc.). This book will serve as your guide in preparing for the CompTIA A+ exam.

The A+ Certification

This is a certification program developed by CompTIA (Computer Technology Industry Association). This program is designed to provide a consistent way of checking the competency of computer technicians. The A+ certificate is given to people who have reached the degree of knowledge and diagnostic skills required to give proper support in the PC industry.

The A+ certification is similar to other programs in the industry (e.g. Microsoft Certified Systems Engineer and Novell's Certified Novel Engineer). The principle behind these certification programs is that if you need to get services for their products, you want to find technicians who have been certified by these programs.

The Benefits of Being A+ Certified

There are many reasons to get your own A+ certification. The information packet distributed by CompTIA gives the following benefits:

- It serves as a proof of your professional achievement.
- It improves your marketability.
- It gives you excellent advancement opportunities.
- It is now considered as a requirement for other kinds of advanced computer training.
- It encourages customers to do business with you

How to Become Certified

The A+ certification is given to anyone who passes the exams. You are not required to work for any company. CompTIA is not a secret group or society. It is, on the other hand, a group of elite computer technicians. If you want to be A+ certified, you have to do these things:

- Pass the exam called A+ Essentials
- Pass one of the three technician examinations:

- IT Technician Test
- Depot Technician Test
- Remote Support Technician Test

You can take the tests at any Pearson VUE or Thompson Prometric testing center. If you will pass both exams, you will receive a mail from CompTIA. That letter will inform you that you passed the tests. Additionally, it contains the certificate, a lapel pin, and a business card.

How to Sign Up for the Exams

To sign up for the tests, you may call Pearson VUE at 1-877-551-7587 or register online at www.vue.com. For Thompson Prometric, call 1-800-777-4276 or visit the website www.2test.com.

These companies will ask for your name, employer, phone number, mailing address, and SSN (Social Security Number). If you don't want to give out your SSN, a provisional number will be given to you. Additionally, they will ask when and where you want to take the exam.

Obviously, the exams aren't free. You have to pay your chosen testing company. That means you have to specify the payment arrangement during the registration process. You can simply provide your credit card information to the customer representative you will talk to. If you're doing it online, you can enter the credit card info on their payment page.

Who Should Use This Book?

If you want to pass the A+ tests, and do it confidently, you should use this book as a guide for your preparations. The A+ Essentials test is created to measure basic skills for an entry-level computer technician. The technician tests are designed to certify that you have the required skills to service microcomputer hardware.

This eBook was created with one purpose in mind: to help you pass the A+ exams. This guide will do that by explaining the things on which you will be tested.

Chapter 2: The Different Parts of a Computer

A PC (i.e. personal computer) is a machine made up of different components that work together to perform tasks (e.g. helping you write a document or add up large numbers). With this definition, notice that computers are described as having various distinct parts that work together harmoniously. Nowadays, almost all computers are modular. That is, they possess parts that can be replaced if the owner wants to improve the performance of his device. Each part has a specific purpose. In this chapter, you'll learn about the parts that make up a common PC, how they work, and what their functions are.

Important Note: Unless stated otherwise, the terms "computer" and "PC" can be used interchangeably throughout this eBook.

The Different Parts of a Motherboard

The motherboard, also called the system or planar board, serves as the "spine" of a PC. This is the brown or green circuit board that you'll find at the bottom of your computer. The system board is the most important part of a PC since it houses and/or connects the other parts of a computer together.

<u>*Different Types of Motherboards*</u>

There are two main types of motherboards. These are:

Integrated Motherboards – With this type, most of the parts are integrated into the system board's circuitry. Basically, integrated motherboards are created for simplicity. Since majority of the components are already part of the board itself, you won't have to install them individually. However, this simplicity has a major drawback: once a component stops working, you cannot simply replace it; you have to replace the entire motherboard. These boards are cheap to manufacture but expensive to repair.

Note: If one of the parts breaks, you may just disable it and add an expansion card that has similar capabilities.

Nonintegrated Motherboards – Here, the major parts (e.g. disk controllers, video circuitry, etc.) are installed as expansion cards. You will easily identify this kind of system board since every expansion slot is occupied by a major component.

<u>*The Different Form Factors of Motherboards*</u>

Computer experts also classify motherboards according to their design (also known as *form factor*). Here are the main form factors being used today: NLX, BTX, ATX, and micro ATX. You have to be vigilant when buying a computer case and system board separately. Some cases lack flexibility: they might not accommodate the system board you will select.

Let's discuss each form factor:

1. NLX – This is the abbreviation for "New Low-profile Extended". In general, this form factor is used for cases that are low-profile. With this design, the expansion slots (e.g. PCI, ISA, etc.) are placed on a special card to reduce the vertical space they occupy. Daughter boards, or adapter cards, that are normally plugged vertically into the expansion slots, are placed parallel to the system board. That means their size won't affect that of the computer case.

2. BTX – This form factor was launched by Intel back in 2003. With this design, the head-producing parts are lined up against the power supply's exhaust fan and the air intake vents. Then, the other components are cooled by installing heat sinks on the motherboard. This design offers a quiet setup since it involves efficient airflow paths and fewer exhaust fans.

3. ATX – With ATX motherboards, the processor and memory slots form a 90° angle with the expansion cards. This design places the memory and processor in line with the power supply's exhaust fan. Thus, the processor can remain cool while it runs. In addition, you may add expansion cards (even the full-length ones) to an ATX motherboard since the memory and processor are not parallel to the expansion cards.

4. Micro ATX – This form factor is similar with the previous one, with one major difference: it is designed for smaller computer cases. Micro ATX motherboards benefit from the enhanced cooling designs of their full-sized counterparts. However, since they are smaller, they have lesser motherboard headers, integrated components, expansion slots, and memory modules.

Processors – Their Functions and Characteristics

Now that you are familiar with system boards, you have to learn about their most important part: the central processing unit (CPU). The CPU controls all of the computer's activities using both internal and external buses. Basically, it is a processor chip that contains millions of transistors.

Important Note: Nowadays, the word "chip" describes the whole package that a computer technician may install into a socket. However, this word was originally used to refer to the silicon wafer hidden inside the carrier (i.e. the "chip" you see on your motherboard). The pins that you see on the outer part of the carrier are connected to the silicon wafer's small contacts. These pins allow you to install the carrier into a socket.

You can identify which part inside the PC is the central processing unit: the CPU is a large square that lies flat on the motherboard with a large fan and heat sink.

The Features of Modern Processors

- Hyperthreading – This word refers to HTT (hyper-threading technology). Basically, HTT is a variant of SMT (simultaneous multithreading). This kind of technology uses the scalar architecture of modern CPUs.

  HTT-capable CPUs appear as two different processors to the computer's operating system (OS). Because of this, the OS may assign two processes simultaneously, such as symmetric multi-processing, where multiple processors utilize the same network resources. Actually, the OS should support SMP in order to use HTT. If a process fails because of missing information caused by, for instance, branch prediction problems, the processor's execution resources can be reassigned for a different procedure that can be conducted immediately. Thus, the processor's downtime is dramatically reduced.

- Multicore – A CPU that has a multicore design contains two processors inside the same package. Here, the OS may treat the CPU as if it were two different CPUs. Just like the HTT, the OS should support SMP. Additionally, SMP is not considered as an upgrade if the apps run on the SMP system are not meant for parallel processes. A good example for the multicore technology is the i7 Quad-Core Processor from Intel.

- Microcode – This is the group of instructions (also called instruction set) that compose the different microprograms that the CPU executes as it performs its functions. The MMX (multimedia extensions) is a special example of an individual microprogram that performs a specific instruction set. Basically, microcodes are at a lower level than the codes used in computer programs. On average, each instruction from a computer program requires a large number of microinstructions. Intel and other processor manufacturers incorporate the MMX instruction set into their products.

- Overclocking – This feature allows you to increase the performance of your CPU, on par with processors created to function at overclocked rates. However, unlike processors created to function on that speed, you have to make sure that the overclocked processor doesn't damage itself from the increased level of heat. You might need to install an advanced cooling system (e.g. liquid cooling) to protect the CPU and other computer parts.

- Throttling – Processor throttling, also called clamping, is the process that specifies the CPU time to be spent on a computer program. By specifying how individual programs use the processor, you can "treat" all of the applications fairly. The principle of Application Fairness turns into a major problem for servers, where each program may represent the work of another user. That means fairness to computer programs becomes fairness to the users (i.e. the actual customers). Customers of modern terminal servers take advantage of this feature.

Memory – Its Functions and Characteristics

Nowadays, memory is one of the easy, popular, and inexpensive methods to enhance a computer. While the computer's processor runs, it stores data in the machine's memory. Basically, the more memory a machine has, the faster it can operate.

To determine the memory of a computer, search for thin sets of small circuit boards that are packed together near the CPU. These circuit boards sit vertically on the computer's motherboard.

How to Check for Errors in a Computer's Memory

Parity Checking

This is a basic scheme used to check for errors. It lines up the computer chips in a single column and separates them into equal bit groups. These bits are numbered beginning at zero. All of the number *x* bits, one from every chip, create a numerical array. If you are using "even parity", for instance, you will count up the number of bits contained in the array. If the total number is even, you will set the parity bit to zero since the bit count is already even. If the total is an odd number, on the other hand, you should set the parity bit to 1 in order to even up the bit count.

This technique is effective in identifying the existence of errors in the arrays of bits. However, it cannot indicate the location of the errors and how to solve them. Keep in mind that this isn't error correction – it is just a simple error check.

ECC

ECC stands for *Error Checking and Correcting*. If the computer's memory supports this method, the system will generate and store check bits. Whenever the machine accesses its memory, an algorithm will be performed on the check bits. If the result turns out to be zero (or a group of zeros), the information contained in the memory is considered valid and the computer functions as normal. ECC can identify single-bit and double-bit errors. However, it can only correct errors that are single-bit in nature.

The Four Main Types of Memory

- DRAM – This is perhaps the most popular type of RAM out there. DRAM stands for *Dynamic Random Access Memory*. Because of their inherent simplicity, these memory chips are cheap and easy to create compared to the other types. This kind of memory is called dynamic since it needs constant update signals in order to keep storing the data written there. If the DRAM chips won't receive stable signals, the information they hold will be deleted.
- SRAM – This stands for *Static Random Access Memory*. Unlike DRAMs, this kind of memory doesn't require a steady stream of signals. In general, SRAM chips are more complex and expensive than DRAMs. You can use SRAM for cache functions.
- ROM – This is the abbreviation for Read-Only Memory. It is called as such because it prevents the user from editing the memory it contains. Once the data is written on the computer's ROM, it cannot be changed anymore. ROM is usually used to hold the machine's BIOS, since this data is rarely modified.
- CMOS – This is a special type of memory chip. It is designed to hold the configuration settings of a computer's BIOS. CMOS is battery-powered: that means the configuration is retained even if the machine is turned off.

Storage Devices – Their Functions and Characteristics

Computers are useless if they can't store anything. Storage devices hold the information being used, as well as the programs and files the computer needs in order to function properly. In general, storage devices are classified according to their capacity, access time, and physical attributes.

HDD Systems

HDD stands for *Hard Disk Drive*. This storage device is also called hard disk or hard drive. Computers use HDDs to allow quick access to data as well as permanent storage. Typically, hard disks are found inside a computer.

An HDD system is composed of:

Controller – This component controls the storage. It knows how the drive functions, emits signals to the different motors inside the disk, and accepts signals from the sensors within the drive. Nowadays, hard disk manufacturers place the drive and controller in one enclosure.

Hard Disk – This acts as the physical warehouse for the data. HDD systems store data on little disks (about 3-5 inches in diameter) grouped together and kept inside an enclosure.

Host Adapter – This is the system's translator: it converts signals from the controller and hard disk to signals the computer can work with. Most modern motherboards have a built-in host adapter, allowing drive cable connection through board headers.

Floppy Drives

Floppy disks are magnetic storage devices that use plastic diskettes enclosed in a tough casing. Several years ago, floppy disks were used to easily transfer information from one computer to another. Nowadays, few people are using floppy disks because of their small capacity. DVD-ROMs and CD-ROMs have replaced floppy disks in storing and transferring digital information.

CD-ROM Drives

Modern computers use CD-ROM drives. These compact disks are virtually similar to those used in music recording. CD-ROMs allow you to store data for a long period of time. In general, these drives are read-only: you cannot erase or delete the data once it is stored on a CD. In addition, computers need to spend a longer time in "reading" CDs compared to internal hard drives. Why are these drives so popular?

Despite their drawbacks, CD-ROMs are used because they can store large files (about 650MB) and are extremely portable.

DVD-ROM Drives

This is the newest storage device to be used for computers. The DVD (i.e. digital video disc) technology is mostly used for entertainment purposes (e.g. home theater systems). DVD-ROMs are basically similar to the DVDs you use at home. Because of this, computers that are equipped with a DVD-ROM drive can play movies stored on a DVD.

However, DVD-ROMs are way much more useful when used for computers. Since they use newer technology, DVD-ROMs are better than CD-ROMs in terms of storage capacity. On average, DVDs can hold 4GB of data. That means DVD-ROMs are your best option if you are storing or distributing large files.

Important Note: CD-ROMs and DVD-ROMs have the same appearance. The single difference is the logo on the front of DVD drives.

Removable Storage Devices

Many years ago, the term "removable storage" meant something extremely different from what it means now. Tape backup is one of the old storage devices that can still be bought today. Modern computer users prefer the solid-state, random-access removable storage devices. In this section, you'll learn about tape backups and the new storage solutions.

Tape Backup

This is an old type of removable storage. A tape backup device can be installed externally or internally and utilize either an analog or digital magnetic tape to store data. In general, this kind of device can hold more information than other storage mediums. However, they are also one of the slowest in terms of data transfer rate. Because of these reasons, tape backup devices are mainly used for archived information.

Flash Memory

Before, random-access memory chips were only used to access and use data. But now, you'll find them in different physical sizes and storage capacities. Flash memory drives are considered as the best solid-state storage device available. The flash memory category includes SD (secure digital) and other memory cards, USB flash drives, and older detachable and non-detachable memory mechanisms. Each of these storage devices has the capability to store huge amounts of information.

Manufacturers of flash memory devices use revolutionary packaging (e.g. keychain attachments) for their products to provide easy transport options for their end-users.

Chapter 3: How to Work With Computer Parts Effectively

While taking the CompTIA A+ exam, you will answer questions regarding the installation, usage, and replacement of computer parts. This chapter will help you to review regarding those topics.

How to Install, Configure and Optimize Computer Parts

Aside from knowing the characteristics and functions of PC components, you also need to know how to use them. In particular, you should be familiar with the installation, configuration, and optimization of such parts.

How to Upgrade a Storage Device

Storage devices are available in different shapes and sizes. Aside from IDE and SCSI, two of the most popular types, there are SATA (Serial ATA) and PATA (Parallel ATA). You can also differentiate between external and internal drives. This section of the book will explain each of these options.

Preparing the Drive

Regardless of the technology being used, you should format storage devices before using them. Although most drives have their own formatting software, each OS has a tool that you can use. When working with Windows computers, you can utilize the format utility through the command line. If you are working with XP, Vista, 7, or newer Windows system, you can also use the graphical utility program called Disk Management.

How to Work with IDE

Before, IDE (integrated drive electronics) drives were the most popular kind of computer hard drives. Although they are often linked to hard drives, IDE is more than just an interface for hard disks. It can also serve as the interface for different storage types such as Zip, DVD, and CD-ROM.

To install IDE drives, you should:

1. Set the slave/master jumper on the IDE drive.

2. Place the drive inside the drive bay.

3. Connect the cable for power-supply.

4. Link the ribbon cable to the motherboard and to the drive.

5. If the drive isn't detected automatically, you should configure it using the BIOS Setup of your computer.

6. Use your PC's operating system to format and partition the IDE drive.

How to Work with SCSI

SCSI is the abbreviation for *Small Computer System Interface*. This kind of device can be either external or internal to the machine. To configure an SCSI device, you should assign an SCSI ID (also called SCSI address) to all of the devices in the SCSI bus. You can configure their numbers using a jumper or DIP switch.

Whenever the computer sends data to the SCSI device, it emits a signal on the cable assigned to that number. The device will respond with a signal that holds the device's number and the information needed.

You should install a terminator (i.e. terminating resistor device) at the two ends of the bus to keep the SCSI devices working. You can activate and/or deactivate terminators using a jumper.

Here are the things you should do when installing an SCSI device:

- For Internal Devices – Connect the cable (i.e. a 50-wire ribbon cable with multiple keyed connectors) to the adapter and to each SCSI device in your computer. Afterward, place the terminators on the adapter and terminate the final device in the chain. You should leave other devices unterminated.

- For External Devices - Follow the steps outlined above, but here, you should use some stub cables between the SCSI devices in the daisy chain (instead of a long cable that has multiple connectors). Terminate the adapter as well as the final device in the daisy chain (that device should have one stub cable linked to it).

- For Hybrid Devices – Many types of adapters have connectors for external and internal SCSI devices. If you have this kind of adapter, attach the ribbon cable to your internal devices and connect the cable to your adapter. Afterward, daisy-chain the external devices from the external port. Terminate the device at the end of every chain. Make sure that the adapter is unterminated.

External Storage Devices

As capacities shoot up and prices fall down, the number of available external storage devices has increased greatly. Aside from the SCSI variant explained above, you will also see devices with USB connections and those that can connect straight to the system. The computer's operating system will recognize USB devices upon connection. You can just install any additional programs you like to use. A computer program called Dantz Retrospect is included in many storage devices to allow you to utilize external devices as automatic backups.

If the external storage device is linked straight to the system, you can just follow the instructions that came with that product. Then, install additional programs on the computers that you will be using. The main benefit of linking straight to the system is that the storage device/s can be accessed by all of the computers.

How to Upgrade Display Devices

Before linking or unlinking a display device (e.g. a computer monitor), make sure that the computer and the device itself are powered off. Afterward, connect a cable from the computer's video card to the display device. Connect the power cord of that device to an electrical outlet. You may use a modern Digital Visual Interface (DVI) cable or the traditional DB-15 (or VGA) cable.

While installing a new monitor, you should have the proper driver. The driver is the software interface between the display device and the computer's OS. If you don't have the right driver, your monitor won't display what you want to see. Nowadays, you can download the newest drivers from the website of monitor manufacturers.

Aside from the power supply, the most dangerous part to repair is the monitor. Computer technicians say that beginners should never attempt to repair monitors. Monitors can hold high-voltage charges even if they have been powered off for several hours. That means you can be electrocuted if you will try to repair a monitor by yourself. If your monitor stopped working, and you don't want to buy a new one, you should take that device to a TV repair shop or a certified computer technician. The technicians and the repair guys know how to fix monitors properly – they understand the dangers and the correct procedures.

How to upgrade Input and Multimedia Devices

The typical upgrade for input devices is the transition to newer mice and keyboards.

Keyboards

Keyboards may wear out if used repeatedly. The usual problem is "key sticking", where keys are no longer responding to the user. To replace a PS/2 101-key keyboard with a new one, just unplug the old keyboard and plug in the new. As you can see, this is a quick and easy process. Nowadays, however, computer users prefer to replace old keyboards with USB ones.

Here is a principle you need to remember: You can use the "unplug-the-old-and-plug-in-the-new" procedure as long as your computer's OS supports the keyboard you want to use.

Mice

Computer mice also wear out because of repeated use. But don't worry: you can replace old mice with new ones. You may easily replace a PS/2 connection mouse with another without spending too much. As an alternative, you may buy an optical mouse (which prevents dust- and ball-related problems) or a wireless one (which needs batteries to send and receive signals). Although new mouse models still use the PS/2 type of connection, most mouse products in the market use the USB connection.

Chapter 4: The Tools Needed for Checking Computer Parts

The CompTIA A+ exam will also test your skills in checking computer parts. This chapter will help you with that topic by discussing the tools and diagnostic procedures needed.

The Tools Needed by a Computer Technician

A great computer technician needs a great collection of tools. If you are working alone, you may not get past the troubleshooting phase. However, you still need to use certain tools in order to succeed in that task. Once you have identified the problem, you will need to get another set of tools in order to fix it.

This book will focus on the "hardware" tools. These are:

- Screwdrivers – When checking a computer technician's toolkit, you will surely find screwdrivers. Almost all of the big computer parts you'll see today are mounted using screws. If you need to remove these parts, you need to have the right type of screwdriver. This kind of tool is divided into three types:
    - Flat-Blade – Many people refer to this as the *common* or *standard* screwdriver. The screw used with this screwdriver is rarely used today (mainly because the screw's head can be destroyed easily).
    - Phillips – This is perhaps the most popular type of screwdrivers being used today. The screws used with a Phillips screwdriver have enough head surface: you can turn them many times without damaging the screws' head. According to recent reports, more than 90% of the screws used in computers belong to the Phillips-head type.
    - Torx – This is the type of screwdriver you use while working on tiny screws found on Apple and Compaq computers. The screws you remove using a Torx screwdriver have the most surface to work against: they offer the best resistance in terms of screw-head damage. Nowadays, Torx-type screws are gaining more popularity because of their clean and technical look.
- Flashlight – This is one of the tools you should always have. You'll realize how important this tool is when you're crawling under a table searching for a dropped computer part.

- Needle-Nose Pliers – You should have this in your toolkit. This kind of pliers is great for holding connectors or tiny screws (particularly if you have large hands). If needle-nose pliers are still too big to do certain tasks, you may use a pair of tweezers.

- Compressed Air – While working on a computer, you will usually remove the machine's case first. Once the cover is removed, it would be great if you will clean the computer's internal components. The clumps of dirt and fibers can block airflow inside the system unit. As a result, the PC's life will be shortened. The ideal way to eliminate the dust is by using compressed air.

  If you are working for a big company, you probably have a core air compressor that supplies compressed air. If this kind of compressor is not available, you may purchase canned compressed air. However, you'll be shelling out large amounts of money – cans of compressed air are expensive.

- Soldering Iron – You can use it to splice broken wires. Nowadays, computer technicians rarely use this tool. Here's the reason: modern computer parts are created with quick-disconnect connectors. You can easily replace them without splicing anything.

- Wire Strippers – Whenever you have to solder something, you need to use a stripper/wire cutter to prepare the wires for connection. Stripping means you will expose a certain part of the wire by removing the insulation.

- Multi-Meters – This tool is named as such because it is basically a set of different types of testing meters, such as ammeter, voltmeter, and ohmmeter. When used by a trained technician, a multi-meter can identify the failure of various types of computer parts.

  A multi-meter has an analog or digital display, a mode selector switch, and two probes. You can use the switch to perform two things: (1) select the function you want to test and (2) choose the range in which the meter will work. If you need to use an old meter to measure a power pack, you should manually set the range selector. Modern multi-meters, particularly the digital ones, can automatically find the correct ranges.

  Important Note: You should never measure voltage by connecting a manual ranging multi-meter to an AC electrical outlet. This will damage the meter itself, the meter mechanisms, or both.

<u>How to Measure Resistance Using a Multi-Meter</u>

Resistance is the property of electricity commonly measured when troubleshooting computer parts. This electrical property is measured in ohms and represented by the Greek letter "omega." If a multi-meter indicates infinite resistance, the electric currents cannot travel from one prove to another. If you are using a multi-meter to check the resistance and you are getting an infinite reading, there's a huge possibility that the wire is broken.

When measuring resistance, you should set the tool to measure ohms. You can do it using either the selector dial or the front button. Then, connect the PC component you want to measure between the tool's probes. The multi-meter will then show the component's resistance value.

<u>How to Measure Voltage Using a Multi-Meter</u>

This process is similar to the one discussed above, but with two main differences:

1. While measuring voltage, make sure that you properly connect each probe to the source of electricity. For DC voltage, the "-" should be connected to the negative side and the "+" to the positive one. This positioning is irrelevant when measuring AC voltage.

2. You should switch the selector to Volts DC (VDC) or Volts AC (VAC), depending on what you need to measure, to instruct the tool about the voltage you are working with. These settings protect the tool from overload. The multi-meter will blow up if you will plug it into a power source while it's still on "measure resistance" mode.

Chapter 5: Operating Systems

The CompTIA A+ examination will test your knowledge regarding operating systems. Since operating systems play an important role in the computer industry, you should be familiar with them. This chapter will guide you in this topic. Here, you'll learn different things about a computer's OS.

What is an Operating System?

Computers are useless if they don't have any piece of software. Well, you can use them as a doorstop or paperweight – but that is not cost-efficient. You need to have an interface before you can use the capabilities of a computer. And, if you don't know yet, software acts as the interface. Although there are different kinds of software, or computer programs, the most important one you'll ever need is the OS.

Operating systems have various functions, most of which are extremely complex. However, two functions are critical:

1. Interfacing with the computer's hardware

2. Providing an environment in which other pieces of software can run.

Here are the three main types of software that you will encounter in the CompTIA exam:

- Operating System – It provides a stable environment for other computer programs. In addition, it allows the user to enter and execute commands. The operating system gives the user an interface so they can enter commands (i.e. input) and get results or feedback (i.e. output). For this, the OS should communicate with the PC's hardware and conduct the tasks below:
    - Device access
    - Output format
    - Memory management
    - File and disk management

  Once the operating system has performed these basic tasks, the user can enter instructions to the computer using an input device (e.g. a mouse or keyboard). Some of the commands are pre-installed in the operating system, whereas others are given using certain applications. The OS serves as the platform on which the PC's hardware, other pieces of software, and the user work together.

- Application – This is used to complete a specific task. Basically, an application is a computer program written to support the commands given to the OS. Every application is compiled or configured for the operating system it will be used for. Because of this, the application depends on the OS to perform most of its basic functions.

  When a program accesses the computer's memory and linked devices, it sends a request to the OS. The machine's operating system will perform the requests made by the program being used. This setup helps greatly in decreasing the programming overhead, since most of the executable codes are shared – they are written onto the operating system and can be used by different applications installed on the computer.

- Driver – This is an extremely specific program created to instruct an operating system on how to access and use a piece of hardware (e.g. webcam, flash memory, etc.). Every webcam or flash memory has distinct features and settings – the driver helps the OS in knowing how the new hardware works and the things it can do.

The Terms and Concepts Related to Operating Systems

In this section, let's define some of the most important terms and concepts. Study this section carefully since it will teach you the terms you'll encounter during the CompTIA A+ exam.

Key Terms

- Source – This is the code that explains how computer programs work. An operating system can be open source or closed source.
  - Open Source – The users have the right to change and examine the code.
  - Closed Source – The users are not allowed to edit or check the code.
- Version – This is a specific variant of a computer program, usually expressed by a number, which informs users regarding the "newness" of the software. For instance, MS-DOS is now in its sixth main version. Computer programmers distinguish minor revisions from major ones this way:
  - "Program" 4.0 to "Program" 5.0 is a major revision.
  - "Program" 5.0 to "Program" 5.2 is a minor revision.

- Shell – A piece of software that works on top of the operating system. It allows users to execute commands through an array of menus or a different type of graphical interface. A shell makes an operating system simpler and easier to use by modifying the GUI (graphical user interface).
- GUI – The method by which a user communicates with computers. A GUI uses a touchpad, mouse, or a different mechanism (aside from a keyboard) to interact with the machine and issue commands.
- Multithreading – The capability of a computer program to contain several requests in the computer's CPU. Since it allows an application to perform different tasks simultaneously, computers experience a boost in performance and efficiency.
- Network – A group of computers that are connected by a communication link. A network allows computers to share resources and information.
- Preemptive Multitasking – This is a multitasking technique in which the operating system allocates each program a certain amount of CPU time. Afterward, the OS takes back the control and provides another task or program access to the CPU. Basically, if a computer program crashes, the operating system takes the processor from the faulty program and gives it to the next one (which must be working). Even though unstable computer programs still get locked, only the affected application will stop – not the whole machine.
- Cooperative Multitasking – This is a multitasking technique that relies on the applications themselves. Here, each program is responsible for utilizing and giving up access to the CPU. Windows 3.1 used this method to manage multiple programs. If an application stalls while it is using the CPU, the application fails to free the CPU properly, and the whole computer gets locked, the user needs to reboot the machine.

Conclusion

Thank you again for purchasing this book!

I hope this book was able to help you to prepare for the CompTIA A+ tests.

The next step is to reread this book and use other information sources. That way, you can increase your chances of passing the exam.

Finally, if you enjoyed this book, please take the time to share your thoughts and post a review on Amazon. It'd be greatly appreciated!

Thank you and good luck!

www.ingramcontent.com/pod-product-compliance
Lightning Source LLC
Chambersburg PA
CBHW060929050326
40689CB00013B/3020
* 9 7 8 1 5 2 3 8 6 7 0 5 9 *